"Did I Ever Tell You About When You Were Little?"

Deborah Shaw Lewis and Gregg Lewis

ZondervanPublishingHouse
Grand Rapids, Michigan

A Division of HarperCollins*Publishers*

"Did I Ever Tell You About When You Were Little?"
Copyright © 1994 by Deborah Shaw Lewis and Gregg Lewis

Zondervan Publishing House
Grand Rapids, Michigan 49530

Library of Congress Cataloging-in-Publication Data

Lewis, Deborah Shaw, 1951–
    "Did I ever tell you about when you were little?" : building togetherness and values
  by sharing stories about your family / by Deborah Shaw Lewis and Gregg Lewis.
    p. cm. — (Family share together)
  ISBN 0-310-41071-1 (softcover)
  1. Family—Anecdotes. 2. Parent and child—Anecdotes. 3. Storytelling. 4. Family—
Folklore. 5. Oral biography. I. Lewis, Gregg A. II. Title. III. Series: Lewis,
Deborah Shaw, 1951– Family share-together book.
HQ518.L482 1994   94-32891
306.85—dc20   CIP

Illustrations by Liz Conrad

Printed in the United States of America

94 95 96 97 98 99 / ❖ CH / 6 5 4 3 2 1

Welcome to the Adventure of Storytelling!

When I was growing up, my parents told me the story of the time I almost died. I was two months old when I became sick. Mother called the doctor, but it was Friday and he couldn't see me. He listened to my mother's description of my illness over the phone and assured her that I just had a cold. She shouldn't worry.

On Saturday I got worse. I seemed better on Sunday morning when my father left to preach at his student pastorate. But by the time he arrived home late that afternoon, he found my mother rocking me and crying. My fever had reached 107 degrees.

They took me to the hospital. The doctor who examined me angrily informed my parents that I was dying of pneumonia—that there was "no hope." And he used strong language to tell them that it was their fault for not bringing me to the hospital earlier.

The doctor left my grief-stricken parents in the waiting room while he did what he could to save me. My father called some friends at the college he was attending. Those friends gathered for an all-night prayer vigil in the chapel at Asbury College, praying for a two-month-old baby girl they hardly knew.

One of my lungs collapsed. I lay night and day in an oxygen tent. When I finally began to recover, even that crusty old doctor who had cursed at my parents called it "a miracle."

Time and again as I grew up, my father would tell me that story. Then he would tell me the story of John Wesley, the founder of Methodism, who as a small child was miraculously saved from a burning house. And Daddy would tell me that I, like John Wesley, was a "brand plucked from the burning," that God had saved my life for a special purpose. And I believed him. All of my growing-up years, I was confident that I was a special child of God, that he had preserved my life because he had plans for me.

Experts tell us preschool children spend twenty-one hours per week watching television and older children an amazing thirty-five hours per week! This means millions of children today learn about life from their favorite television shows. In comparison to the people he sees on television, your child must feel ordinary. After all, he cannot fly, change size, turn into a dinosaur, or run faster than the speed of sound. And he doesn't get to start life with a fresh slate, after every half-hour episode.

But when we tell our child a story about himself, he is the main character, the star, the hero. Through the story both parent and child focus on who this child is. Your child hears one of these messages: "I am a person of value, who is smart . . . giving . . . kind . . . curious . . . independent . . . a hard worker . . . a good helper . . . worthy. And I am loved and valued by the people who know me best."

Such positive, affirming input may be especially important for teenagers. Most teenage rebellion is rooted in the very natural and normal quest for the answer to that basic and age-old adolescent question: "Who am I really?" Many teens, in their pursuit of independence and a new adult identity, try for a time to cast off their childhood identity, pull away from old relationships, and sometimes even reject the values their parents tried so hard and so long to instill in them. Some teens very deliberately try out new identities that seem almost opposite of what they were like as young children. And in a phenomenon that threatens to drive some parents crazy, most teenagers can seem like peripatetic pendulums swinging wildly back and forth between the most basic childlike behavior and this new adult identity they're trying to find.

We, as the parents of two teens (the time will come when we will have four at one time), have already learned there are no simple parenting strategies for surviving adolescence. But we find family storytelling a helpful tool.

The morning of his thirteenth birthday, after the family had sung "Happy Birthday" to him, Matthew sat on the side of our bed and grinned sheepishly as his siblings laughed at one of our favorite Matthew stories.

"I remember eleven years ago today when I had baked and decorated a very special 'Cookie Monster' cake to celebrate your second birthday. You were so excited," I said.

"It was almost noon when I said, 'It's your birthday, Matthew. What would you like for lunch today?'

" 'I want birthday cake,' you said.

" 'Not yet, honey. We're saving that for supper,' I said. And you pouted.

" 'But you can pick what we have for lunch today because it's your birthday,' I said, trying to cheer you up. 'So, Matthew, what would you like for lunch? Anything you want.'

" 'I'll have supper,' you replied, and began to grin.

"Even at two years old you were a creative person with a good sense of humor."

Matthew and his older brother Andrew sometimes roll their eyes in mock embarrassment when we retell "cute" stories about their childhood. But they honestly enjoy hearing them. And we keep telling them in the hopes they will serve as reminders and affirmation of the special individuals they are and always have been. Just maybe the stories will somehow lessen the swing of that adolescent pendulum and help them build their adult identity on the foundation that's already there.

Each time a story is told about a child, his place in the family is reaffirmed. At the same time, his parents remember who he was as a little child and are reminded of how he is growing and maturing.

Family storytelling may be one of the most positive and powerful parenting tools. It is certainly a memorable and special gift you can give your children. Each time you tell a family story, you have given them your time, attention, and a piece of yourself.

Family storytelling is also an adventure. Each family takes its own twists and turns down the path, discovering a heritage uniquely its own. The purpose of this book is to encourage you to begin that adventure with your family by helping you and your children to remember when they were little.

Maybe you're reading this and thinking, "I'm no storyteller! My kids wouldn't want to listen to me." Or, "I wouldn't know where to start. Nothing remarkable or interesting ever happened in our family. Besides, I've got such a terrible memory I've forgotten the details."

Then keep reading! The rest of this book will be especially helpful for anyone who feels he or she has no family stories to tell. While it may be true that most of us will never be great storytellers, every family has stories worth telling. And every child deserves and needs to hear stories from his life remembered and recounted. Every child ought to have the chance to be the "star."

So we've designed the remainder of this book to help parents search their minds and memories to build a repertoire of stories from the episodes of their children's lives. Our "Story Starters" and

"Storytelling Tips" include a hodgepodge, bushel-basket full of story-related questions, suggestions, and comments to consider. You might want to think of them as a computer menu for calling up the files of your memory, or as a set of keys to unlock the doors of your own rambling house of recollections.

Some entries on a computer menu are seldom used. A few keys on our old key rings no longer open any doors. In the same way, not all of the following material will effectively trigger your memories. But some of them will. And when they do, when you start telling your children stories about when they were little, you will have begun your own great adventure of family storytelling.

*Tell your child about
the day she was born.*

- Tell what you had been doing before the birth.
- Tell the details of the birth—day of the week, the trip to the hospital, the people involved, and how long you were in labor.
- Tell about how you found out you were pregnant, how you felt, and what you did in preparation.
- Tell how you felt when the baby was born, the first time you held her, and what she looked like.
- How did you tell your family about your new baby? What did they say?

In some stories, children are reminded of talents or positive character traits; in others, mischievousness or stubbornness; and in others, forgiveness and acceptance. We tell our son Andrew that as he entered the world, he cried just once. Then he began looking around, his eyes wide open and alert. He examined each of our faces intently. "I knew even then," I tell Andrew, "that you were very observant." He still is.

*If your child was adopted,
describe the day you first saw him.*

- Where was he?
- What did he look like?
- How old was he?
- What events led up to the adoption?
- Who were the people who helped with the adoption?
- What were you doing when you got the phone call telling you that the baby was ready?
- How did you feel?
- What did others in the family say when they heard the news?

When we tell our child a story about himself, we build his sense of identity and help him to see himself as a part of a family and as a part of God's design. As he listens, your child is hearing more than just a story. He is hearing that, in this story, he is the main character, the star, the hero. And because he has a unique place in your family, the events of his life are indeed worth telling about and remembering.

Tell about the day your child came home from the hospital.

- Who came to welcome you home that day?
- How old was your child?
- Did someone come and stay to help out for several days?
- Did you stay with someone else for a few days?
- How did your baby sleep? Eat? Cry?
- Who came to see the new baby?
- What special, silly, or useless baby gifts did you receive?

Details are important to make a story interesting and colorful. Any details you can remember add to the visual picture. Make sure your child knows the names and ages of the other people who are in the story. Describe what the people looked like and what they were wearing. Details add to the story and give children a frame of reference.

Did your child have a special toy he liked to sleep with—a teddy bear, stuffed animal, or doll? Tell him about it.

In his bestselling book, *How to Really Love Your Child*, psychologist Ross Campbell says children need four things from their parents to feel truly loved: eye contact, physical affection, focused attention, and discipline. Eye contact and physical affection usually come easily once parents realize their importance, and most of us find discipline to be inevitable. Focused attention, however, is tougher in that it often requires that parents examine their priorities and make a serious sacrificial commitment of time to their children.

Family storytelling provides an excellent time of focused attention. And when the stories are told about your children, they receive a double dose of esteem-building attention.

*What was the first word
your child said?*

- Tell about something funny or interesting your child said.
- Did she have favorite words that she mispronounced?
- Did she ever say anything awkward or embarrassing?

At a recent family gathering my sister Beth told her daughter Amanda a story. When Amanda was two years old, her older brother Josh went through a period of frequent ear infections, accompanied by very high fevers. Beth spent most of one day sitting with Josh, feeling his forehead, and worrying out loud. "Oh, you are really hot, Josh!" And, "I think you're getting hotter."

Apparently Amanda was feeling a little neglected. She approached her mother, hand to her own forehead, and said, "Mama, I hot on top, too!"

After Beth finished the story, Amanda commented, "I was an adorable little kid!"

"You still are!" her mother added, looking up at her tall daughter. "Just not so little!"

Jonathan and Lillian

Our youngest son, Jonathan, has a same-age cousin Lillian, who lives in the same town we do. Lillian stayed at our house during the day, while her mother worked outside the home, from the time she was two years old until she started kindergarten this past year.

Lillian came for a visit recently. That evening seemed to be a good occasion for some Jonathan and Lillian stories. Here is one of them.

One day we were driving down the road toward our house. Lillian, age two, was very verbal and talked in long sentences. Jonathan was two months younger than Lillian and could talk pretty well. But he also babbled sometimes, like a baby does—making sounds just for the fun of making sounds.

Well, I had their car seats arranged so that they were facing each other in the van. And Jonathan was babbling, "Wa-wa-la-la-tah-tah-doo-doo-loo-loo."

Lillian turned to me. "Aunt Debi, Jonathan said, 'Doo-doo'!"

At first I tried to ignore it.

"Ba-ba-da-da-doo-doo-doo-doo!" said Jonathan.

"Aunt Debi!" Lillian said, louder, "Jonathan said, 'Doo-doo'!" She was clearly appalled that I would allow such language in my car.

"Lillian," I explained, "Jonathan is still a little boy. And he is just playing with some sounds. He doesn't mean to say anything bad."

"Da-da-doo-doo-da-da-doo-doo," said Jonathan.

"Aunt Debi!" said Lillian, even louder. "Jonathan said, 'DOO-DOO'!"

"He's just a little boy, and he's just playing with sounds," I said again.

Now, Jonathan may not have been as verbal as Lillian, but he is pretty smart. By that time, he had clearly figured out that the "doo-doo" part of what he was saying meant something. I stopped the car and turned around to look at him. He was leaning forward in his car seat, looking right at Lillian and saying loudly, "DOO-DOO-DOO-DOO-DOO-DOO-DOO-DOO!"

In their book *The Blessing*, Gary Smalley and John Trent urge parents to "picture a special future" for their child as one part of giving a child a "blessing." In each storytelling session, you can look for ways to do that. You might ask your child what he will do with his own children. You may want to comment, "I could tell even when you were little that you were good with animals. You might be a veterinarian one day." Or, "You are so good with babies. I know you will be a good father (or mother) one day."

*Describe the first home
your child lived in.*

- Tell a funny anecdote about your child that you associate with that house.
- What family routines do you remember from your time there?
- Tell the address and what the house looked like.
- Did you have a baby nursery? How was it decorated?
- Where in that house did your baby play? How long did you live there? How old was your child when you moved away?

In our mind's computer, many of our memories are filed by the places in which they occurred. Remembering places is a powerful way to unlock the doors of our minds. As you tell your children about a place in their past, often the memories of events and people associated with that place will flow, as if a door has been opened. Out of those places and details, stories may grow.

Tell a funny story about getting your child dressed one day.

- Did she have clothes that she loved or hated to wear?
- Tell about when she was learning to dress herself.
- Or can you think of a funny story about your child's bath time? Or about changing her diaper?

If I close my eyes and imagine walking into the door of the house where we lived when Andrew and Matthew were babies, I find memories. I picture that couch and remember the afternoons Andrew and I napped there together. If I imagine walking into the kitchen, I remember the morning Andrew ate a box of dry chocolate pudding and tried to hide the evidence.

Taking a walk through your home, in your imagination, is an exercise that may awaken memories for you, too.

Tell a story of a funny mealtime incident with your child.

- Did he ever turn the bowl upside down on his head . . . or throw his food to the floor? Tell about games you played to get him to eat.
- Describe your mealtime routines.

Family gatherings are places to ask questions, learn new family stories, and fill in the details when our own memories are incomplete. When I see my mother, I sometimes ask her to tell her version of certain stories. She remembers details I have forgotten. And the children enjoy hearing her tell the stories, too.

*Tell about a special memory
you have of bedtime
when your child was little.*

- What was your family bedtime routine? Did your child fall asleep nursing, crying, quietly, or while being rocked?
- How many hours did your child sleep as a tiny baby?
- How old was she when she first slept through the night?
- Tell about naptime, naptime routines, or bedtime routines.

Lisette the Engineer

On one tape we enjoy listening to, Southern storyteller Kathryn Tucker Windham talks about how her mother fixed grits every morning for breakfast. She recounts all the ways grits could be fixed. She talks for five or six minutes about grits. The story that follows is what we call a "grits" story. It is a collection of interesting facts, thoughts, and memories about a single subject. In this case, the subject is a specific aspect of Lisette's character. Here is the story as I sometimes tell it to the whole family or as I would tell it to entertain Lisette's friends.

Lisette is my engineer. She has always loved to figure out how things work. She had hardly learned how to walk when she figured out how to make the buzzer on the stove go off. As a baby she would turn the jack-in-the-box around and upside down, trying to figure out what made it pop.

She carefully examined and studied all her toys. I remember the day she discovered how to take the bottom off her busy-box and got so that she could make the figures pop up by pushing the right part underneath. Was I surprised! The internal mechanisms were different for each one of those pop-up people. But she knew just where to push each one of the five.

Even as a baby, she would pull the bath mat up at the corners and study the little suction cups that held it down. She would run her fingers around the edge of the suction cup, push it down and pull it up again, frown, and look at it intently.

And while the water was running into the bathtub, she would watch it come out of the faucet. And when I turned the water off, she would twist her head around to look up into the faucet. It was as if she were trying to figure out the connection between the water, the faucet, and the knobs to turn it off and on.

I suppose her interest in seeing underneath things and inside things was behind her episode with the wallpaper.

She was only eighteen months old. We were selling our house on Arapahoe Trail—the green house with dark green shutters. And, with three small children, I was having a terrible time keeping the house clean enough to show to prospective buyers.

One day, at the end of nap time, I heard Lisette talking to herself. I went in to check on her and there she was, sitting up in her bed, picking the wallpaper off the wall! She had removed a large portion—several inches high and a foot or so wide—and torn it into little bitty pieces. She was having a wonderful time!

Well, she had damaged two sections of wallpaper. And we didn't have any more of that style. So we had to re-wallpaper the entire room.

We had the new wallpaper up and, oh, that room looked so pretty! It had been finished for three, maybe four, days, when I went in during nap time again. There was Lisette, sitting up in bed, picking at the new wallpaper!

I went out and got another roll of wallpaper. But I didn't put it up. I just left the roll, with the sales receipt, in Lisette's closet. It's a good thing I didn't worry about it. The family that bought the house had two sons. One of the first things they did was paper that room with boyish wallpaper!

But Lisette still likes to figure out how things work. She likes to

use the pump to put air into her bike tires. She likes to scribble on one place on her Etch-a-Sketch. That way she can see the wires on the inside and examine how the Etch-a-Sketch works. And she sometimes studies the hand brakes on her bike and the scooter. I'm just waiting for the day when she can repair everyone's bikes.

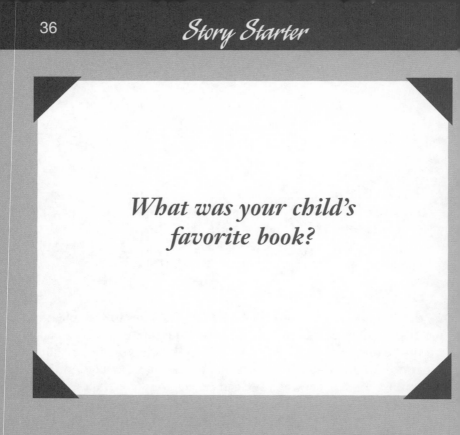

What was your child's favorite book?

- How old was your child when you began reading to him?
- Did he have a book he wanted to read over and over?
- What was your family storytelling routine?
- Tell the story of the time something funny or unusual happened at story time.
- What other books did your child enjoy, as he got older?

*Tell about the time
your child began to crawl.*

- How old was she?
- Did she scoot on her belly first? Or roll to get where she wanted to go?
- Did she move fast or was she cautious?
- Tell about the time she got into mischief while crawling.

Do not wait until your story is "perfect" to tell it. No one is a "perfect" storyteller, and very few people are master storytellers. Most of us stumble around a bit as we tell stories, especially the first few times, but children are very forgiving audiences. And, with practice, you will become a better storyteller, and your children will become more experienced listeners.

Tell about the day your child took his first steps.

- How old was he?
- Who was there at the time?
- Did he walk carefully, go fast, or fall down?
- Now, tell about the time he used his new-found locomotion to do something or go somewhere unexpected.

When my niece Hannah first learned to walk, she discovered a new pastime. She could walk to the table, get her parents' keys, take them to the bathroom, and drop them into the toilet. What fun for Hannah!

What was the most memorable time your child deliberately disobeyed you?

- How old was he?
- How did you find out?
- How did you discipline him?
- What did you learn from the experience?
- What do you think he learned?

> *Often when we remember what it was like when our children were little, one episode stands out in our minds: something cute our son said, or some mischief that our daughter got into. That story is a good place to start.*

Benjamin and His No's

This is one of my favorite Benjamin stories. This is a full-blown story: one I have thought through, dramatized, and told a number of times. Consider working up at least one such story for each of your children.

Right after Andrew left for school one morning, the year Andrew was in first grade and Benjamin was not quite two years old, Benjamin found my purse and brought it to me saying, "Gum, Mama?" Now, believe it or not, he could chew gum (half a stick).

"Not right now, Benjamin. It's too early in the morning," I told him. I took my purse and put it on the kitchen counter, out of his reach. (You see, I knew from past experience that "no" is not enough. One must also remove temptation.)

So, Benjamin stomped off and, oh! you should have seen him stomp! *(Here I demonstrate stomping.)* And I went in the other direction—I was trying to ignore Benjamin's temper tantrum.

One minute later, I heard the sound of CRASH, thud-dump . . . CRASH, thud-dump. So I raced into the kitchen to find Benjamin,

red-faced, jaws clenched, picking up a plastic bowl, raising it over his head, and throwing it to the floor. *(I act out the motions.)* There were eight or nine bowls strewn across the floor!

Of course the plastic bowls were in the cabinet under the counter upon which I had put my purse. But I wasn't surprised. Benjamin has always been a very determined person.

One day we were visiting my mother. The older children were playing in the backyard. Mother and I were in the living room talking. And Benjamin, who was nineteen or twenty months old, was playing alone in the family room.

Mother got up to check on Benjamin. She came back and motioned for me to follow her. *(I demonstrate a beckoning motion.)* And she shushed me. *(I put my finger to my lips.)*

I followed her as we tiptoed to the door of the family room. She and I listened, while Benjamin . . . all alone . . . said, "NO! No-o-o-o? No. NO! No." *(With each word, I use a different volume or tone.)*

"Debi," my mother said, "you are going to have your hands full with that child! He's practicing his no's!"

We need to make memories with our children. Since our oldest son, Andrew, was three years old, Gregg has taken each of our children out to eat breakfast on his or her birthday. On the drive to the restaurant he always retells his story of the day they were born. And while they eat breakfast, one of the questions he asks them is this: "What has happened to you this year that you think you will remember when you are an adult? Tell me about it."

Each parent can look at their schedule and brainstorm ways in which to incorporate such family times into their lives. One father devotes his Sunday afternoons to his children, at least one half-hour alone with each child. Another mother walks around a local hiking path with her daughter after gymnastics class each week. Many of our best stories come from these special times we spend with our children.

Tell your older child about the day his younger brother or sister was born.

- Who took care of her while the new baby was being born?
- Did she attend any big-sister classes before the birth?
- How did she react to the new baby?
- Tell about the time she was angry with her brother or sister. Or about the time when she got her brother or sister's goat.

Before our fourth child, Benjamin, was born, Andrew announced one day that I was expecting triplets. "Andrew, what makes you think that?" I asked.

"I prayed for triplets. And God always answers prayer," Andrew answered.

I told him, "Yes, God answers prayer. But, thank goodness, he doesn't always say yes!"

*In what ways did your child
help around the house
when he was little?*

- What was the first chore you asked your child to do? How old was she at the time?
- Which ones did she like to do? Which ones did she dislike?
- Did she ever refuse to help?
- How did her chores change as she got older?
- Describe a time when she made a mistake while trying to help around the house. Tell about a funny incident that happened while she was doing chores.

You want your child to feel loved and accepted, even when he has failed. So tell about the times he messed up, as well as the times he succeeded. Children need to be reminded that no one is perfect and that they are loved even when they are not heroes.

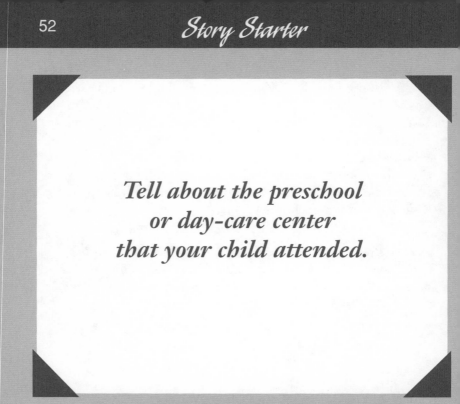

*Tell about the preschool
or day-care center
that your child attended.*

- What was the name of the place?
- How old was your child when he began to go there?
- Who were his teachers?
- What funny story or special memories do you associate with his days in preschool?
- What toys did he like to play with there? Which activities were his favorites?

While it's valuable to have the whole family present for some storytelling sessions, times alone with each child are essential, too. So while you are scheduling time to tell stories to your children as a group, also plan for and set aside time alone with each child.

*Tell about a time
when your child lost something
that was important to her or broke
something that couldn't be fixed.*

We've purposely focused most of our story-starter questions on the positive aspects of relationships. But we're well aware that some of these questions may elicit powerful emotions for children and parents. There's more to be said about the therapeutic value of storytelling in such instances than can go into this book. But story-telling can be an effective means of opening communication lines with your children regarding sensitive issues. Not only can you learn what your children are thinking and feeling, but you can also help correct misunderstandings you never realized existed.

*Tell about the first
big purchase your child made.*

- When did he begin receiving an allowance?
- How much money did he get?
- How did he spend his money? In what store?
  What did he buy?
- Did he have to think about it a long time?
  Or was it an impulse buy?
- What did you learn about your child as a result?

*Tell the story of how
your child learned to ride a bike.*

- What did the bike look like?
- Did she have training wheels first?
- Did she fall down in the process?
- Now tell about when she learned to roller-skate, swim, or tie shoes.

*Tell the story of your child's
first day of kindergarten.*

- Who was her teacher?
- Was she happy to go to school, or did she cry?
- Did she know another child in the classroom?
- Did she walk to school, ride a bus, or ride in a car?
- Did you walk her into the school?
- How did you feel that day?

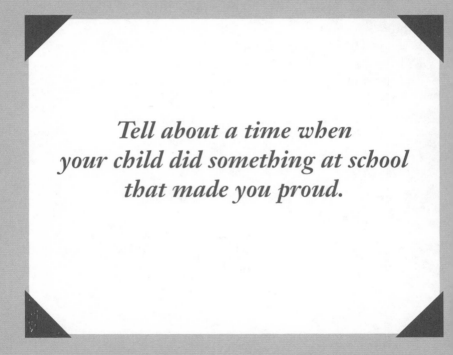

*Tell about a time when
your child did something at school
that made you proud.*

- How old was he? What grade was he in?
- What did you say to your child to let him know that you were proud?
- Tell your child something positive a teacher said about him.
- What other incident reminds you of that character trait in your child?

Whenever you tell about an event or a person, set the story into a specific time and place. If you begin with, "When you were four years old and we lived in our house with red shutters . . . ," your listener will have a framework for visualizing the setting for the story.

*Tell your child about a day
when he was little
that didn't turn out
the way you expected it to.*

- What did you have planned for that day?
- How did your plans begin to go wrong?
- What other people were there?
- What did your child do either to help or hinder your plans?
- Describe the rest of the day.

Each time we tell a story, the repetition jogs our memories, and we remember another detail to add. Or we think of another way to fill the story out, to make it more dramatic, or to involve our children in the story. And each story you tell will remind you of another incident in your child's life, giving you another story to tell.

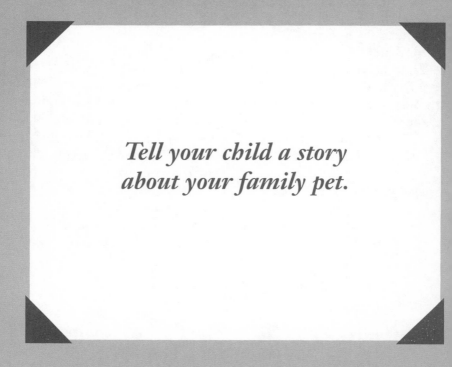

*Tell your child a story
about your family pet.*

- How old was your child when you got the pet?
- What kind of animal was it and what was its name?
- How did your child respond to the animal?
- What was their relationship?
- What memorable story do you associate with that pet and your child?

Anytime you are telling a story about an event your child might remember, always ask her if she remembers it, too. Let her add her memories and her perspective to your story. You may be surprised at the details that she will remember. And then the next time you tell that story, you can incorporate some of her memories as a part of the tale.

*Tell about a time when
your child did something
dangerous or frightening.*

Often as we remember stories about our children, we describe only what we saw. As you compile stories about your children, think about the other four senses, too. What smell do you associate with each memory? What sounds, especially music? How did someone or something feel to the touch? What tastes or foods do you think of when you remember a person, place, or event? Sensory details add texture and flavor to your stories. Try to include two or more kinds of sensory memories in every story you tell.

*Tell about a time when
your child was sick or injured.*

- How did she hurt herself—or how was she sick?
- Did she have stitches or a cast?
- Did she see a doctor, or go to the hospital?
- Were you worried or frightened for your child?

Helping Children Tell Their Own Stories

Parents should not be the only family storytellers. For when we listen to our children tell their own stories, we learn more than we could imagine about who they are and what they are thinking. We've found such value in this that we've created new family traditions that allow us time to listen to our children's stories.

When my husband, Gregg, is gone on business trips, one of my favorite things to do is to take my children to a local Chinese restaurant. After ordering, we go around the table, and each person has to tell something funny that has happened to him in the last week.

This tradition began as a means of entertaining the children so that they would behave in the restaurant. But it has developed into a wonderful time of sharing, during which I gain meaningful insights into what my children are thinking and how they are perceiving the current events of their lives.

By setting aside a block of unhurried time, we establish an

atmosphere in which the children have time to relax, open up, and begin talking about things that are important to them. Teenagers in particular usually need extra time to lower the normal barriers of adolescent reluctance and reserve. So it's important to be patient and not try to rush either a story or its teller.

I've also learned over the years that when a child is telling a story about himself, it's crucial for me as the parent to be an active, interested listener. The child should be the one in control of the story. You can ask questions, encourage your child to give more details, and show interest and empathy. But you must also be careful to let the child be the storyteller.

Children, like adults, don't become eager or accomplished storytellers overnight. It takes time and repetition. But if you start early and keep at it, you'll be pleasantly surprised at the results.

The following "Story Starters" and "Storytelling Tips" are included specifically for parents to use in encouraging children to tell their own stories. But they may also trigger memories parents can tell about their children's early years.

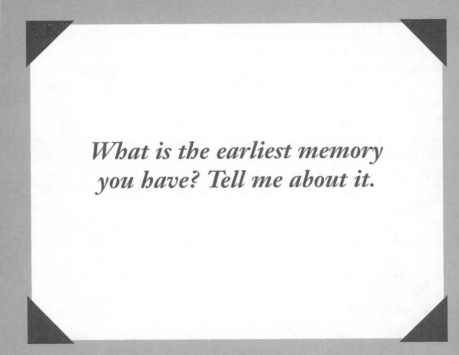

*What is the earliest memory
you have? Tell me about it.*

- Where were we living then? Describe that first house as you remember it. What did your room look like?
- What did the kitchen look like? The family room? Where did you sit while we told you a story or read you a book?
- Describe the yard where you played.
- Tell us about something funny, sad, or unusual that happened while we were living there.
- What do you remember about the neighborhood we lived in?
- Tell about a trip we made into town.

In their book, Unlocking the Secrets of Your Childhood Memories, *Kevin Leman and Randy Carlson build a convincing case for the significance of a person's earliest memories. They say such memories provide great insight into what is important to a person, what the person is really like, and how the person perceives himself today. At the very least, asking your children to recount their earliest memories may result in some surprising stories that will enrich your family storytelling times.*

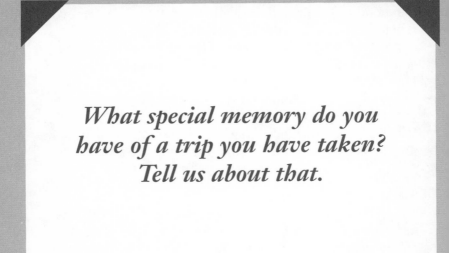

What special memory do you have of a trip you have taken? Tell us about that.

- Where did you go?
- What did you like about the trip?
- What is the first (best, worst, or most memorable) vacation trip you remember our family taking? Where did we go on the trip?
- Tell us what you remember about the first time you traveled on an airplane or a train.
- Name a relative—grandparent, aunt, uncle, or cousin—whom you enjoyed visiting.
- Have we ever gone on a vacation that became an adventure?

You can personalize many of these questions. Rather than saying, "Tell about a trip," ask, "What do you remember about the trip we made to Kentucky when you were six?" By adding personal details, your questions may elicit more memories and more stories.

*Remember a day
when you had a really good time
with your mother or father.*

- Where did you go and what did you do?
- Did anyone else go along?
- Do you think this is something you would like to do with one of your children when you grow up?
- Now tell about a good time you had with your brother or sister.

> *When children are learning to tell stories, they will often skip details, tell things in a disorganized way, or condense events. Help them flesh out their stories by saying, "Paint me a picture of what was going on." Or, "Give me a play-by-play account. Tell me what happened first, then what happened next."*

Tell us about your first friend.

- What was her name?
- Which house did you live in when you knew her?
- How and where did you meet her?
- What games did you play with her?
- Who else played with the two of you?
- Tell us about a time when the two of you got into trouble.

Some children tell long, involved stories. Others will answer one or two words to each question, and you'll feel like you're pulling teeth to get a story out of them. Just give them more time and attention, and they'll open up. Don't ask too many questions, but ask enough to let them know that you are interested in their stories.

Do you remember one especially good birthday? Tell us what was so memorable about it.

- How old were you?
- What made it so special?
- Who came to the party?
- What gift do you remember receiving?
- Now tell us a story about a disappointing birthday.

Tell us about your favorite Christmas.

- What do we do at Christmas that you like?
- Has there ever been a time when we did something different for Christmas?
- What holiday traditions does our family observe that you want to do with your own children?
- Tell about something unusual or memorable that happened at Christmas.
- What special foods do we have just at Christmas?
- What do you like about visiting your grandparents during the holidays?
- What special things do we do at your grandparents' house?
- Tell what you like about other holidays: Halloween, Fourth of July, Valentine's Day, or Thanksgiving.

The Kindergarten Runaway

When Andrew was in kindergarten, he ran away from school one afternoon. He walked all the way home by himself and hid in the bushes at the front of our house. When I saw him there, I was startled. Then I was frightened: he could have been hurt or kidnapped on that long walk alone. And I was angry: "Don't you ever do anything that dangerous again!" I said. After a stern talking, I sent him up to his room.

Several years later, I told the story of that day. Then Andrew told his version:

The day I ran away from kindergarten was my first day as a Christian. It was in Spring, on a day in May. I don't remember the exact date.

I had just been dropped off at school. I walked up to the school. When I opened the door, I jogged to my homeroom. I put my coat on the outside rack.

I heard the door to the room open. I ducked behind the coats so I wouldn't be seen. I saw the attendance helper go down the hall.

I got scared, because I knew the consequences for being late.

The moment she was out of sight, I got my coat and left. My house was within walking distance of the school. I don't remember what was going through my mind.

I knew I was in trouble when I came home. I told my parents what had happened and why I came home. I remember crying a little bit. About an hour of crying.

I went to my parents' room to be by myself. I was still crying when it came to my mind. That's when I prayed for the Lord to come into my heart.

After that I felt different and felt renewed. I had been to church since I was born, but this was a new kind of feeling that I had never felt before.

Each time Andrew tells that story, he remembers a detail he hadn't remembered before. And in the telling, he reaffirms the choice he made that day. And we all remember how adventuresome he is.

*Tell us the story
of your first day of school.*

- Were you frightened, worried, or excited about going? Did you cry, get sick, or misbehave?
- Did one of us walk you into the room?
- What do you remember about your first teacher? What was her name? Did you ever get into trouble with her? When did you do something that was fun or special?

Story Starter

*What has been your
favorite year in school so far?
Tell what you liked best about it.*

- Tell about a time when a teacher encouraged you. Or tell us about a time when a teacher was unfair.
- Tell us about the principal you wish you could see again.
- What subject in school do you like the most?
- What subject gives you the most trouble?
- What special privileges have you had in school? Doing school patrols or being a crossing guard? Classroom monitor? A part in the school play? Playing in the school band?
- What's the funniest thing you remember ever happening at school? Or the scariest? Or the most unusual?

Children should never be pressured to answer a question that makes them feel uncomfortable. If a question doesn't click with your child, simply move on to another question.

*Remember a time
when you were very angry.*

- Who made you angry? A friend, brother, sister, or parent? What had they done?
- How old were you then?
- How did you work things out?
- Now tell about a time when you made someone else mad.
- And remember a time you got into a lot of trouble with your father or mother.

*Tell us about a day
when you were afraid.*

- What had happened to frighten you?
- Who was with you? Who comforted you?
- Now remember a day when you were sad, lonely, angry, embarrassed, worried, or shy. Tell us about that day.
- Now tell us about a time when you did something that made your mother and father proud of you.

*Tell us about playing T-ball
(or softball, soccer,
football, gymnastics, etc.).*

- Have you ever been the team hero?
- Have you ever let the team down?
- What did you play?
- What was the most memorable game you took part in?
- Tell us about the coach and the other players.

*Tell us about your earliest
memory of something
that happened at church.*

- Was it something funny or unexpected?
- Were you misbehaving in church?
- Who is your favorite Sunday school teacher and why?
- Tell us about your worst Sunday school experience.
- What do you remember about . . . (ask about the programs offered by your church).

*Tell us about a day
when you had an adventure.*

- How old were you at the time? What happened?
- Tell about the time you got lost or separated from your family.
- Recount the most traumatic event that has ever happened to you.
- Recall some big plans you had that didn't turn out at all like you'd expected.
- Remember a time when your guardian angel must have been watching over you.

Wilbur the Dragon

When our two oldest sons were little, Gregg often made up bedtime stories in which they were the heroes. These stories highlighted some positive attribute we'd seen in the boys or some trait we wanted them to value and develop—like loyalty, friendship, kindness, ingenuity.

As author Ron Rose says in his book, Seven Things Kids Never Forget, *"Creating your own stories for your children connects you emotionally with them and allows you to share the values you hold most dear." And it's a fun way to broaden the concept of family storytelling.*

Here's one example our children enjoyed.

Once upon a time there were two brothers named Andrew and Matthew. They lived next door to their best friend, a young dragon by the name of Wilbur.

One day, when Andrew and Matthew were gone on a trip with their parents, Wilbur was feeling particularly lonely. He couldn't think of anything he wanted to do. So he was very excited when his mother came home from the mall and said, "I got you a surprise, Wilbur."

And she handed him a shopping bag.

He looked inside. There in the bottom of that bag was the biggest red balloon he'd ever seen.

"Can I blow it up?" he asked.

"Sure," his mother told him. "But you better take it outside because it's awfully big."

So Wilbur went outside with the bag and carefully unfolded the big balloon. Fortunately dragons have a lot of hot air, because this was the biggest balloon Wilbur had ever seen.

He started to blow it up. Whoo. Whoo. Whoo. (*More blowing sounds.*) In just a few breaths it was as big as a basketball. Then as big as a beach ball. Next thing Wilbur knew it was almost as big as he was! And he kept right on blowing. (*More blowing sounds and arm stretching gestures.*) It got bigger and bigger and bigger, until that red balloon was as big as Wilbur's house. And Wilbur was so winded that he had to stop blowing and just hold the balloon tightly in his teeth while he caught his breath.

Now Wilbur had been huffing and puffing so hard that he

hadn't heard his little sister Wilma walk up behind him. So when she tapped him on the back he jumped and gasped in surprise. And when he gasped he opened his mouth just enough that his teeth lost their grip on that balloon and *pshooooooooooooooooooooo*! All the hot air in that balloon came whooshing out.

The trouble was, all the air that he'd worked so hard to blow into that balloon went right into Wilbur's mouth, and before he thought to close his lips, his body had filled with so much air that he was now as big as his house!

And that was just the time a little gust of breeze came up and started him drifting slowly off his patio toward the fence separating the dragon's property from Andrew's and Matthew's backyard.

"Whoa-ooooooo," Wilbur called helplessly as his sister ran screaming inside to get their mother. And then a bigger gust of wind came along and bounced Wilbur up and over the fence, where an updraft started the dragon rising higher and higher.

"Wilbur Dragon, you come back down here right now," his mother called when she ran out into their backyard.

"I caaan't!" Wilbur replied as he rose higher and higher and his voice sounded farther and farther away. Before he knew it, Wilbur had risen almost as high as the clouds. And he was very scared.

Now about this same time Andrew and Matthew were returning to town in an airplane. As the plane circled for its final approach, Andrew spotted a strangely familiar green object in the sky. "Look, Matthew!" he said. "Did you see that? That looks like Wilbur!"

This story continues in too much detail to include it all here. But eventually the boys pull Wilbur down with their kite, then stick a needle in his tail to let the air out of his body. Wilbur is back to normal size and grateful to his good friends, whose problem-solving skills make them instant heroes.

And Andrew and Matthew go on to new bedtime adventures helping other friends in crisis—Elmer the Elephant, whose terrible case of the hiccups shook the ground so much that no one wanted to be around him, and Harvey the Hippo, who got stuck in the mouth of a cave until the boys figured out an ingenious way to free him.

Photo albums are a wonderful way to jog your memory or to give your child a starting place for his own stories. As you reminisce over the photos, your children will love to see pictures of themselves and their brothers or sisters as young children. And looking through photographs, you will remember more stories to tell.

You can begin a story by asking yourself or your child:

- Who are the people in the photo?
- How old was your child at the time?
- What was happening on the day the photo was taken?
- What is the story behind the photograph?
- What else happened that wasn't captured on film?

Adjectives can be powerful memory triggers. Think of adjectives that describe your child. Then begin a story by saying, "You were such a cute (or precocious, mischievous, curious, careful, or whatever) little person. I remember one time when you . . ."

Then go on to recount an episode that illustrates the adjective you had in mind.

"Did I Ever Tell You About . . ."

L ast March our home state of Georgia had its first true blizzard in recorded history. My husband, Gregg, and our seven-year-old son, Benjamin, were stranded at my mother's house in Atlanta. Our four other children and I were marooned in our own home, with no electricity or water. Several hundred trees had fallen across the roads between our house and town. So my children and I had an intense six days together, huddled for hours at a time in front of the fireplace. We spent a lot of that time telling stories.

I told my children stories about their grandparents, me, their father, and them. And then they told me their own stories: tales about family vacations they enjoyed; accounts of their first days of school; Andrew's story of the day he ran away from school.

We did little other than keep warm, learn to cook over a fireplace, haul water from neighbors, and tell stories. After six days, we regained our electrical power, Gregg and Benjamin were home, life returned to almost normal, and Lisette cried. "Can't we spent just one more night camping out in front of the fireplace?" she begged.

It shouldn't take a storm-of-the-century to persuade us to find time for storytelling or to discover how important it is to tell our children stories about themselves. Family storytelling has traditionally taught family values and family identity. In a culture marked by so many fractured family relationships and in a mobile society that has eroded our concept of the extended family, storytelling can strengthen ties too easily broken or lost. Incorporated into the routine of family life, it can lay the foundation for a lifetime of open, honest communication between you and your children.

Family stories about your children carry added potential, for they not only help kids establish a sense of belonging and connection, but they can provide a solid foundation of affirmation and self-esteem.

We trust that as you have been reading this book, you have begun experimenting with telling your children stories. One nice thing about a list of questions like we've included in this book is that you can use it again and again with different results. A quick one-time read-through may trigger one layer of especially memorable details and stories. If you do the same thing again a month from now, your mind will make some new memory connections. And if you really take some time and pick just two or three questions to think about, you'll often uncover additional stories and details that neither you nor your children remembered the first time through.

Each time you tell stories about your children, to your children, the stories will get better. And each time your children tell a story, they too will become better storytellers. They will put events into understandable order and remember to include details that help make their stories more interesting.

And as you use this book, we hope you have lots of fun, because family storytelling should be enjoyable—both for you and for your children. If it's not fun, slow down. It takes time for stories to come together, for families to develop the habit of telling stories.

As you tell family stories to your children, it will indeed become a habit, woven into the very fabric of your relationships with each other. Your children will think to ask for family stories more often. And you'll find yourself regularly asking, "Did I ever tell you about . . ."

Enter the Creating Family Memories Contest!

Do you have a family story to share? It could get you published! Or send you on a family vacation of a lifetime!

Here's How. Write out your favorite family story and mail it to the address below. Your story will be judged on its originality and on how well the event created a lasting memory or drew your family together. The story must be original and not previously published, typed or neatly handwritten, and 500 words or less.

The Prizes. The ten best stories will be published in *Christian Parenting* ($100 value). Grand prize is a six-day, five-night family vacation for four to anywhere in the continental United States. The contest is cosponsored by USAir and Holiday Inn.

Mail in your story with your name, address, and phone number to: Creating Family Memories, Attn. Betty Wood B16, Zondervan Publishing House, Grand Rapids, MI 49530.

The Official Rules. No purchase necessary. Ten winners will be published in *Christian Parenting* magazine ($100 value). One grand prize consists of six days, five nights at a Holiday Inn, round-trip airfare on USAir, rental car, and $200 spending money, for a total $2,500 value. No cash substitute. Entries must be received by March 31, 1995. Judging will be conducted by a panel, and its decisions shall be final. Sponsor not responsible for lost or damaged mail. Taxes are winners' responsibility. All entries become the property of sponsor. The contest is open to residents of the United States, 21 years and older. All prizes will be awarded. Employees or their family members of Zondervan, Family Bookstores, HarperCollins, or their advertising affiliates may not enter. A list of prize winners may be obtained after July 31, 1995 by sending a self-addressed, stamped envelope to the address listed above.